AF375500

Let's Count!

Baby Arizona Animals

By Sharon Roe & Alyssa Bouwens Roe

To Kayeson: may the
numbers in this book
be the beginning of
a lifelong adventure of
learning and love. Hugs
& Kisses-
S.R. & A.B.R.

1

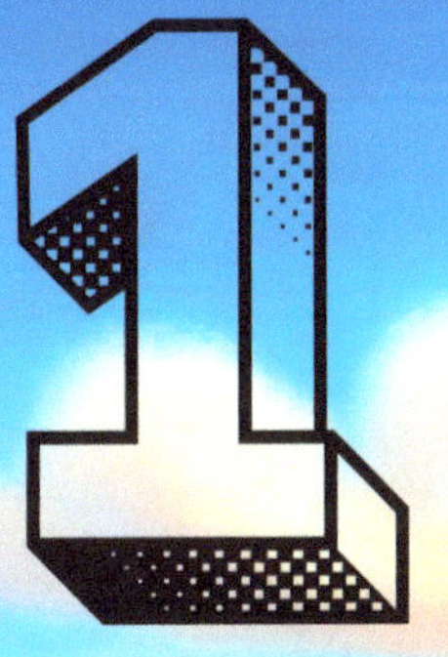

**One baby tortoise
in the desert sun.**

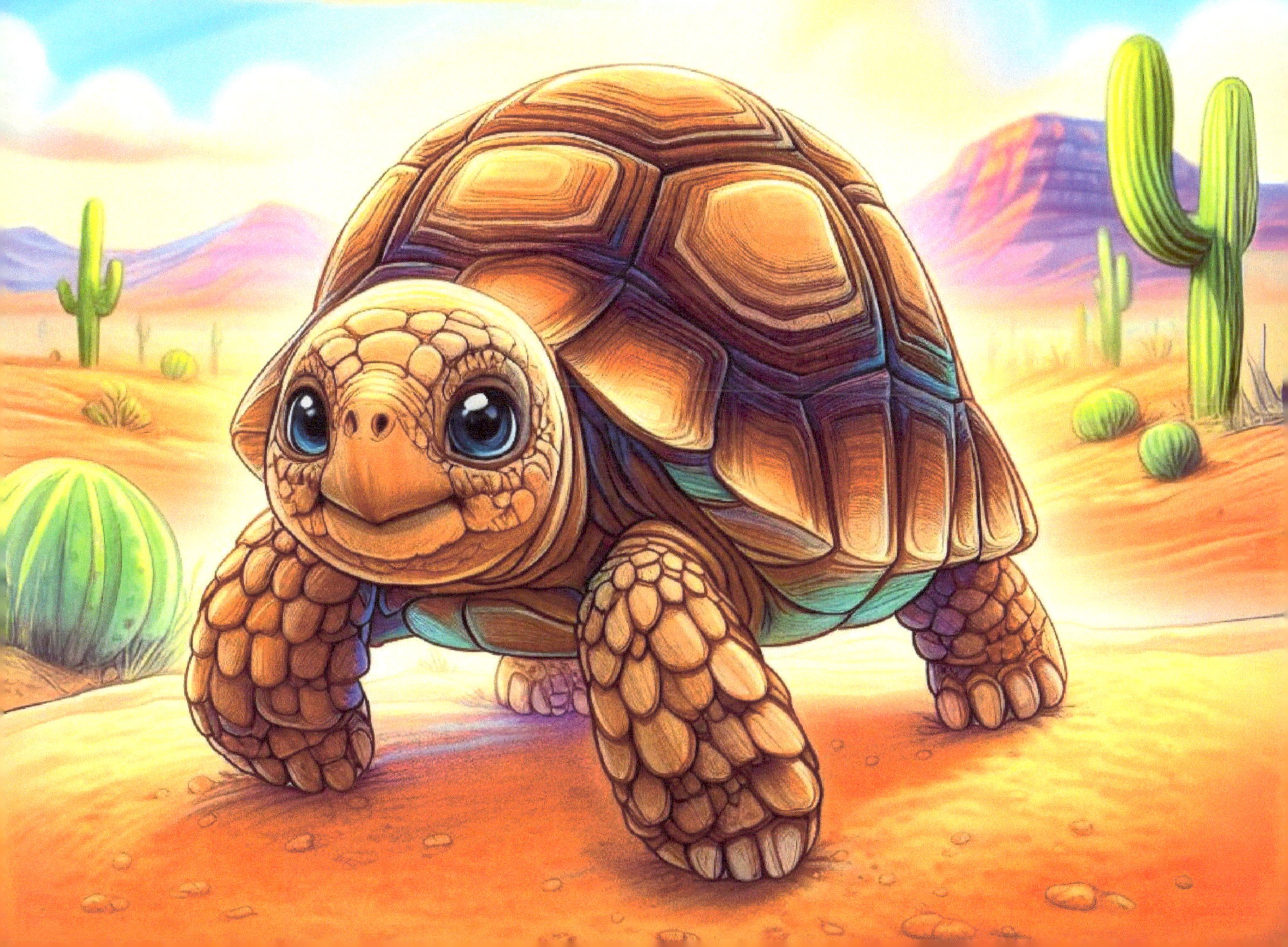

2 Two baby kit foxes always having fun.

3 Three roadrunners racing under the sky.

4
Four baby owls
learning
how to fly.

5
Five
baby bobcats
curled up in their den.

6
Six lizards hanging with their friends.

7
Seven jackrabbits hopping so high.

8
Eight coyote pups, howling beneath the sky.

9
Nine little javelinas,
wagging their tails.

10
Ten Quail parading
on the desert trail.

Now we've counted
up to 10,
Arizona baby animals,
what a happy end!

Let's learn a little more...

Desert Tortoise

They can go a year without water, by storing it in their bladder!

Kit Fox

They have big ears to help them hear tiny sounds in the desert, like insects!

Road Runner

They're speedy birds and can go up to 20 miles per hour and they say "beep-beep"!

Burrowing Owl

One of the only owls that live in burrows in the ground, borrowing from prairie dogs. These tiny owls come out in the day!

Bobcat

They can weigh 15-30 pounds and they're great at climbing trees and catching small creatures!

Eastern Collared Lizard

They can leap 5 times their body length to escape or catch insects!

Jackrabbit

Black-tailed jackrabbits have long ears and legs that make them the fastest hoppers in the desert!

Coyote

Coyotes are clever creatures that love to sing at night with their howls and yips!

Javelina

Javelinas look like pigs, but they are actually peccaries that love to stick together in a family group!

Gambel's Quail

Gambel's quail can run really fast on their strong legs and even fly for a short time with their speedy wings! They also live in flocks or family groups.

Sonoran Desert Toad

Arizona's largest toad and can weigh up to 2 pounds! They have poison glands behind their eyes, so no touching these toxic toads!

Desert Kangaroo Rat

They resemble small kangaroos with big feet and long tails, but they are the size of a mouse. They dont need water- they get moisture from seeds.